SMART WOMEN
STUPID BOOKS

Stop Reading
And Learn To Love Losers

by
Lisa Ann Marsoli and Mel Green

PRICE STERN SLOAN, INC.

To Emilio and Amelia Marsoli, America's favorite couple.

—LAM

To Wilbur and Kathleen Green, my favorite couple.

—MG

Illustrations by Jeanne Bradshaw
Cover design by Steve Wilson Design

Copyright © 1987 by Lisa Ann Marsoli and Mel Green
Illustration copyright © 1987 by Price Stern Sloan, Inc.
Published by Price Stern Sloan, Inc.
360 North La Cienega Boulevard, Los Angeles, California 90048
Printed in the United States of America. All rights reserved.

ISBN: 0-8431-4706-7

TABLE OF CONTENTS

INTRODUCTION

It's not your fault! Men are stupid and smart women know it. It's time to stop worrying and start enjoying them for what they are—which will always be less than you want. This book welcomes you to the age of the "user friendly relationship." Come on, ladies, most everyone has something you can use: a car, condo, cash, two hands. Why not go for it? Are you getting any younger? Are men getting any better? Keep these questions in mind as you read further and discover how you can utilize that inferior partner rather than discard him.

You are probably wondering what makes two chiropractors experts on the psychology of relationships. As a married couple sharing a joint practice, we found that the stress of being an over-achieving couple forced us, and our vertebrae, apart. We have seen beautiful women with I.Q.s and incomes over 140 *twisted* like strands of angry linguine. Contorted backs, fallen arches, ragged cuticles . . . these are the signs of trying too hard!

For example, Beatrice V., 22, had just graduated from a prestigious women's college with a B.A. in industrial design. She stood poised on the brink of becoming a young Over-achieving woman (Ow) of the eighties. She wanted to "do it all and do it right." Like any good student she assembled her "library for life." Books telling her how to dress for success and still know how to make love to a man. Books telling her how to play games mother never taught her, how to be a one-minute manager and a sixty-second gourmet, how to love—but not too much. When Beatrice came to us, covered in paper cuts, her index finger painfully cramped from flipping through book after book—she had reached the end of her rope. The terror of making a mistake (any mistake) as she embarked on her adult life so overwhelmed her that she enrolled in graduate school.

Beatrice and her plight shed light on our own horrible relationship. For months we had been trying to achieve a perfect marriage through the book of the month club.

We finally realized that the enormous goals we set for ourselves were too ambitious to include each other. And that's all right! We were too busy to have a relationship with anyone as busy as us.

When our accountant informed us that separating our practices would be the financial ruin of both of us, we decided to lose the marriage and keep the job; "a user friendly relationship" was born. We now maintain a flourishing practice (together) while enjoying the single life (apart), and revel in the pleasures of shallow, emotionally undemanding relationships.

As chiropractors, we felt the responsibility to treat our patients' deeper problems—not just crack their backs and send them out onto the streets. So began the development of our revolutionary behavior-altering techniques. Simple and easy-to-use, our unique method combines mental imaging, or "daydreaming," with a series of short breaks, or "naps."

As you read our book, you may recognize certain patterns of unhealthy and destructive behavior with which you yourself identify—good! That means you're smart! But remember, it is important that you accept yourself for where you are right now—even if that place is a dreary freeway motel outside of Tulsa. You're not going to change anything—you're just going to start enjoying it. It's your life and you can learn to love it when you put into practice the common-sense techniques prescribed in this book—REALLY.

Now take a deep breath, elevate your feet approximately 46.3 degrees above your body, and get ready to experience the self-help book to end them all!

Chapter One

BACK TO THE FUTURE— Over-achievers in History

The Virgin Mary—Founder of the "New" Celibacy • Since the beginning of history, Over-achieving women (Ows) have been ahead of their time. The Immaculate Conception, for example, was the Virgin Mary's answer to safe sex. She was an ambitious woman who wanted a kid, but wasn't taking any chances—lepers were everywhere and some of them wouldn't even tell you.

All mothers want their baby to be the best and the brightest, and what more perfect way to insure that end than to have God be the father? The two came to terms: God would get major publicity, Mary would become a saint and the kid would take the fall.

Once the child was born, Mary knew she would need a practical, down-to-earth kind of guy around. Joseph may not have been a drawing room wit, but he was a good listener and had a great ass, which they often rode. Joseph was excited by the prospect of marrying a younger woman who was on the cutting edge of a potentially hot new religious movement. He loved the fast lane, the high masses, the sermons on the mount—and

those gifts—myrrh, frankincense, cigars and brandy—
were all things Joseph reveled in.

There is a powerful lesson to be learned here—
Joseph was a deadbeat and Mary was famous, but it
worked! Why? Mary didn't expect too much from Joseph
and Joseph didn't care whether Mary was expecting or
not. This couple truly enjoyed that peace that passes
understanding—better known as "the pre-nuptial
agreement."

**Joan of Arc—PMS as a Leadership
Quality** • At the age of seventeen, while traveling
in Nice, Joan read a copy of the Virgin Mary's thought-
provoking autobiography, *The Madonna Complex*. She
knew Mary was on to something, but figured it would
be four or five centuries before the world would go for
another Immaculate Conception. Like Mary before her,
Joan wanted something from God, not a baby—an
army—a big army of MEN.

Why? Because Joan wanted to kick up her heels
and have some fun, not just sit around all day and weave
jute. She wanted to get out, travel, hoist a few, tell some
jokes, kill some infidels! In short, be one of the boys!

With the onset of puberty, Joan had her first bout
with PMS, and realized it could be her best friend—it
could help her realize her dream. When Joan was pre-
menstrual even *God* had to listen. He promised to give
her an army (French) and the first unisex wardrobe
(Italian), if Joan would just shut up and go away.

Joan had a few good days every month in battle,
but not enough to win a crusade. She was slowing down,
and the constant pressure of being a superwoman (sol-
dier, saint *and* virgin) was too much. Something had to

go. Unfortunately, it was Joan. She was captured and burned at the stake for being a witch—when she was really just a little cranky.

Joan leaves us with an all-important lesson: Try to be one of the boys, and eventually you'll get burned.

Sara Lee—Food as a Source of Power • From Eve to Julia Child, Over-achieving women (Ows) have found a source of power in food. Sara Lee was one such woman. Considered unattractive by most men, Sara set about winning their hearts with her sticky buns, her turnovers, her cheesecake. Sara's father was her first captive mouth and she controlled him utterly. Eventually, he became overweight and henpecked by his own daughter. The pattern was set.

Sara would lure men with her tantalizing goodies, then grow shrewish and vengeful as they became fatter and fatter. Finally, when the man of the moment had become little more than a groveling lump of obesity slobbering at her feet, Sara would leave . . . no forwarding address, no kind words, no casserole in the fridge.

Sara's plight was obvious: as her empire of food grew, so did her fame and wealth—and so did her loneliness. How many once-attractive men now languished in eating disorder centers around the world? How many sensitive, but gullible, souls were to die, overweight, custard stains on their clothes and brownies on their breath? How many? For obvious reasons, statistics are impossible to come by.

Sara felt the burden of her guilt, and withdrew into seclusion, where she wrote her final recipes and refused to see anyone but her chief baker, Alice. When she finally lapsed into a coma and died, the autopsy revealed the cause to a shocked world—Sara Lee had starved herself to death! Why? Because she was so busy she forgot to eat—and no one cared enough to remind her.

Sara left us two things:

1. A reminder that being too good at what you do can be a fatal flaw.

2. A great frozen banana cake.

Chapter Two

THE CONVENIENT MAN—
Low-maintenance Relationships for the Woman on the Go

Today's Over-achieving woman (Ow) is often too busy to meet the demands of the perfect relationship with the perfect man—even if she could find him. For example, Jean B., an executive with a chain of active wear emporiums for the elderly, has a typical business day which looks like this:

7:00 am–8:00 am	Workout with private fitness instructor
8:05	Quits smoking
8:30–9:30	Breakfast meeting with CEO of international mortuary franchise
9:45	Staff meeting begins
9:46	Sends out for cigarettes
10:30	Staff meeting ends
10:35–11:00	Returns phone calls missed while attending meeting

11:00–12:00	Sits in for boss at stockholders' meeting
12:05	Makes mental note to call MA (Meetings Anonymous)
12:15–1:30	Working lunch with personal shopper to discuss fall wardrobe
1:35	Flosses teeth
1:36	Reschedules her daughter's birthday
1:37	Conceives, implements and staffs company branch in Malaysia
2:00	Sets up dinner date with Dale P., a tax attorney
2:05	Freshens lipstick
2:10	Sends FAXs, TELEXs, FEDERAL EXPRESSs, SOSs and grocery order
2:30	Argues with V.P. of Sales
3:00	Threatens to resign
3:05	Checks balance in bank account
3:10	Decides to stay
3:20	Cleans paper work on desk
4:00	Breathes deeply into paper bag
5:00	Has drinks with boss to discuss promotion
6:00	Goes home, checks answering machine, showers, dresses for date
7:00	Meets date at restaurant
7:15	Date ends

Why did Jean's date end so quickly? Because Dale, her date, had suffered through an equally grueling day. Neither one of them had the energy to empathize with the other; indeed, by the time the arugula salad arrived,

both had lapsed into a hostile silence as they fidgeted with their prawn forks.

Let's take the same scenario and substitute a convenient man, such as musician and part-time electrician Paul, as Jean's date. Paul, having awakened at 11:30, is well-rested. He spent the early part of the afternoon writing a birthday song for his mother and the latter part re-wiring a friend's lava lamp.

Paul listens attentively to all of Jean's complaints' occasionally interjecting a sympathetic "Oh, wow, really?" Jean unwinds, relaxes and finds herself laughing as she signs the check. Back at her place, Paul fixes a short in her blender as Jean slips into something more expensive.

After some Drambuie and Shiatsu, Jean and Paul share astonishing sex. As Jean falls into a slumber, Paul alphabetizes her entire record collection.

What Jean, and all Over-achieving women, should learn here is *never* to overlook any man no matter how many stupid books tell you he's not worthy of you.

CLOSE RELATIVES

The truly advanced Ow will learn to develop that sixth sense . . . always scanning for possible convenient partners. As you read you will learn that even the most mundane situation can offer possibilities to the watchful. Let's briefly examine the family "get together." It might be Thanksgiving, a Fourth of July barbecue or even a funeral. Look around: you may have a brother-in-law who looks attractive, interested, or maybe just bored. You used to tell your sister that a dog groomer was beneath her, but what you once deemed to be his drawbacks you now perceive as *qualities* . . . a nice touch with comb and clippers and an amazing patience with things that bite. And don't forget, your sister will be flattered by your sudden interest in her husband's work.

What about your aunt's husband? You used to think his job checking pulp vats at the paper mill was about as boring and dead-end as it can get. But now that your life is so filled with career, the possibility of being in bed with a slower metabolism seems restful—almost Zen-like in its emptiness.

If you are fortunate enough to have a stepbrother then be smart enough to use him. Maybe you used to think managing the Angry Steer was a little adolescent for your taste and perhaps he does smell like a bacon-cheeseburger with fries, but, then again, there he is ready to serve you. You may find that food may not be the only fast thing you acquire a new taste for.

It all lends new meaning to the phrase "keep it in the family." Don't forget, as you investigate your relatives you will be surprised at what you may find: cousins, nephews, and remember, they all have *friends*.

THE MARRIED MAN

Some experts argue that marriage was invented by women to make men seem more interesting. Though dating the married man is certainly no guarantee of good companionship, sex or even a ride home, it can be useful to Over-achieving women who are concerned with convenience.

Having a family of his own, the married man is not going to demand too much of your time and attention, neither will he eat much of your food. When he's with you he feels like he is on vacation, so get into it—be his Barbados, his Ixtapa, his Grand Canyon.

If you're considering the married man you are probably wondering where to look. Well, why not right in your own backyard, or at least your neighbor's? Why limit yourself to the traditional cup of sugar when you can borrow a husband or even a son (see the following section).

Many Ows fear guilt will result from sexual involvement with husbands of neighbors or best friends, but that's ridiculous! A little affair on the side pumps fresh blood into a stale marriage that has declined to meals, television and questions concerning the laundry. A dis-

tracted husband also gives your best friend or neighbor a chance to get out and do a little experimenting on her own.

Utilizing the married man is simply a matter of scheduling, discretion and contraception. And remember, the married man you're having an affair with might have been having an affair with someone else if it weren't for you!

THE UNTOUCHABLES

CHRIST • Active nuns have found the perfect solution to dating while maintaining an absorbing career, by making The Man Himself the career—ultimate "total women," as it were.

Sister Maria Lucia Calzone, 43, a Sister of Mercy at the Blatant Wound Convent for fifteen years, shares her handy solution to the work/love conflict:

"Well, I was worried about how I would climb the ladder of success while still maintaining a family life. Becoming a nun seemed like the perfect answer. First of all, I knew my dad would approve of Him—what Italian father wouldn't—except Papa was a little sensitive about all those rumors concerning Jesus and Mary Magdalene. I'd always gone in for Sunday brunch, candles and incense in a big way, so I figured church would be the perfect office for me. The convent is also an ideal solution for those with a clothing budget problem—dressing for success is a snap when you're a sister.

I find the miracle aspect of my vocation extremely attractive. Sure, a lot of guys can give you a bunch of flowers, a diamond ring or, if you're lucky, maybe even a fur coat; but with God, the sky's the limit. You want a new Lamborghini, fluency in five languages, higher cheekbones—you pray hard enough, you get it! And, if you mess up the relationship, it's okay! He forgives you—again and again and again! "

Perhaps Christ is the right choice for you. It has certainly worked for Sister Maria and the millions of working girls like her. Remember: Christ is the ultimate blind date—and you don't have to worry about how it's going to turn out until you die!

DEATH ROW • Like Sister Maria Lucia Calzone, Mindy Q. found herself a fulfilling, low-maintenance relationship—not in the church, but in the slammer. Mindy tells her story:

"I first met Eddie the Fish in a nightclub in the Bronx. I was immediately attracted to his flashy pinstriped suit, white shoes and thick neck. We dated a few times, had some Chianti, a little ziti and a few laughs. The next thing I knew, The Fish was up on three counts of murder one. Now, he's on death row and I'm doing fine. Why? Because I couldn't ask for a nicer guy, or a more convenient love affair. Eddie is totally absorbed with me; when I visit he treats me as if I were the most important person on earth—which is understandable, considering I know where the gun is. Sure there's some danger involved, but Eddie's friends go out of their way to protect me. Besides, the risk of arrest is a small price to pay for a faithful man. This is one relationship I don't have to worry about getting stale unless, of course, the governor stays his execution. Then we might run into some problems. But as it is—I'm doing fine and Eddie's doin' time."

LONG DISTANCE RELATIONSHIPS

Never before has the adage "Absence makes the heart grow fonder" been so true. Long distance relationships are perfect, low-upkeep timesavers. You have a mate, and yet he's not there annoying you with his laundry, his friends, his toenail clippings. Sometimes you just want a little peace, a little privacy—in short you want them to *go away*—here are some men who do, and with luxurious regularity.

MERCENARIES • Katherine, a 28-year-old WAC, came to us with powder burns on her briefcase and a smile on her face. She did not want treatment, but instead had heard about our book and wanted to contribute her story.

"Tell your readers if it's convenience they want, mercenaries are a great way to go. I met Jack while on tour in Saigon. When I saw how beautifully he had applied his camouflage make-up, I asked him to give me some tips to make my eyes look bigger. He did, and as he smudged the last bit of kohl onto my lids, he revealed himself to be a really warm,

sensitive guy—he's crazy about kittens and pup-
pies *and* The Carpenters. I even saw him watching
Donahue once while cleaning his grenade launcher.
When the war ended we went our separate ways—
I went back to the States and Jack to a quick job
in Belfast. We pledged to write, call and see each
other whenever world events allowed. We almost
got together in Grenada, but Jack was so sweet that

when he found out we might be on different sides, he declined the job.

Now my home is Jack's "favorite foxhole" and I've got a wardrobe full of international fatigues that would make Banana Republic green with envy.

Of course, there are some peculiar personality traits a woman's got to get used to. For one thing, you can't even have the slightest argument with him unless you pay cash up front. Also, the faintest noise can send him into action; once the smoke alarm went off in my apartment and Jack shot out every one of the storm windows while desperately trying to radio for air support.

But, like all relationships, you gotta remember the good times—the advantages make it all worthwhile. Mercenaries have endless supplies of currency—dollars, yen, marks, francs, kopeks, camels, and I'm always receiving gifts from around the world. Every time we're reunited I say, 'Is that a gun in your pocket or are you just glad to see me?' It's our little private joke."

FLIGHT ATTENDANTS • Elaine, a 50-year-old anthropologist and weekend writer of romance novels, has enjoyed an active love affair with a male flight attendant for the past ten years. Elaine reveals the secret of their success.

"I met Wayne on a flight to Samoa, where I was going to do follow-up research on the effects of anthropologists on the natives. He was one of the first male flight attendants ever, so his presence on the plane caught my attention—maybe it was his sincere smile or the cute way his apron hugged his buns. I thought Wayne was exceptional at his job, but when he reached over just before landing and stored my tray table, I knew he wanted more than just my empties. When I deplaned, he gave me an extra bag of honey-roasted nuts with his address and locker number written on the side. In

the past decade, I'd say we've seen each other twenty-five, maybe thirty times. Each stopover is longer and more exotic than the last. Wayne is so attentive to the little things—always freshening my drinks, plumping my pillows. And now that we are older, he has been thoughtful enough to install an oxygen mask above the bed that drops during particularly strenuous bouts of lovemaking. He always makes sure mine is securely in place before donning his own. After all these years, I still feel like we're just taking off."

YOUNGER MEN

They're fresh, exuberant, have stamina and are easy to fool. They are, in a word—young. Let's face it, there's no bod like a young bod, and though older men may have more experience, younger men have more time. Another quality that you will notice is the vocabulary, or lack of it, that younger men have. "Wow," "Huh" and "Really" have a charm and simplicity that keeps the conversation basic and allows you time for your own thoughts.

Where to look? Once again, check the neighborhood. The boy next door? Every young man appreciates the experience of an older woman. You can also enjoy the satisfaction of teaching him how to "do it right." Training a young man in the basics of lovemaking is an important contribution to the future of relationships in general, and to yourself in particular.

Let your imagination run wild. Some obvious possibilities should have hit you by now—the pool boy?
Don't have a pool? Hire a strapping youth to begin dig-
ging. Tell him to bring some friends along and serve
them Piña Coladas (they like sweet drinks).

How about the paper boy? Insist that he hand the
paper to you *personally* (always check yourself for news-
print smudges afterward).

As you gain confidence you can become more elaborate. For instance, being a Boy Scout den mother is a great way to get little chores done around the house while keeping your eyes peeled for talent in other areas.

Chapter Three

BREAKING
THE RULES—
Dating the Deranged

Intense, unpredictable or even aberrant behavior can be fun and exciting—as long as you always inform a friend of your whereabouts and assume no financial responsibility for the consequences. In the current rush to find the "perfect man," the lunatic fringe is often overlooked or discarded much too quickly. The following case histories explore several situations, offering pointers on getting the most out of these "kooky" types.

THE MAD ARTIST • When Alyson T., 40, first walked into our office her problem was clearly visible—her head was turned almost forty-five degrees to the right. At first we thought she was just shy, but soon we realized she was locked in this grotesque position. Alyson had spent so much time looking over her shoulder that she had sprained her neck and was unable to move it.

Alyson graduated from an Ivy League University in the early '70s, where she majored in physics and minored in experimental theater. A Doctor of Physics and head of ballistics research at NASA, most of the men she found around her had little interest in the arts or theatre. Alyson yearned to cut loose with someone exciting. Enter Vance L., an intense conceptual artist whom Alyson met at an art opening. She was immediately taken with Vance's fierce gaze and the bones he wore around his neck. When Vance invited her back to his studio she couldn't resist.

His loft was huge, and on first glance, looked like a taxidermist's workshop. There were bits and pieces of stuffed animals everywhere—some covered with paint, others with plaster and automobile parts. It was strange and exciting. Alyson felt she was in some new undiscovered land of the psyche.

Vance poured them a strong, odd-tasting drink made from finely chopped roots. They talked long into the night about art, religion and where to get really fresh bagels. Finally, the conversation depleted, they fell into silence and each other's arms.

Back at NASA, Alyson thought constantly of Vance—as she stood outside the wind tunnel running tests on nose cones, Vance's face would pop into her mind. She couldn't wait until day's end, when she and Vance would boil some roots and make love.

Things took a sudden, bizarre turn, however, when Vance started showing up at her job, demanding some sophisticated piece of missile hardware that he needed for one of his "pieces." It was becoming embarrassing, frightening even—it seemed like the fun was gone.

When Alyson stopped returning Vance's calls, he would come to her house and stand outside her bedroom window, chanting Hopi burial songs. The police made him leave—for the time being. But Alyson always felt as if she was being followed. She would constantly

look over her shoulder and see a glimpse of Vance disappearing in a crowd or ducking into a car wash. That's when she came to us.

After we straightened out her neck, we began to help Alyson understand her problem—which wasn't really a problem at all, just a situation. Alyson had let Vance's eccentric behavior intimidate her. Vance sensed this and played it for all it was worth. If Alyson had only gotten weird back, Vance probably would have come around, and they could still be enjoying each other's company. But she made Vance feel superior in his weirdness, and therefore, in control. She needed to wave a revolver in his face, speak in tongues or shave off her eyebrows. That would keep him off guard.

Dating the deranged is much more fun when you don't run or reject them, but stick it out and really make them wonder. Alyson is now happily dating a part-time mime who dabbles in real estate.

THE SCHIZO—Playing the Field with One Man • Debi B., 34, is the divorced mother of a young daughter, a professional body builder and owner of forty-eight health clubs across the country. She is also a pub-lished poet, and her most recent collection, *Reflections in a Bead of Sweat,* has been a best seller in Thailand for two months. Until she met Earl, Debi had never had an orgasm she didn't fake.

Earl M., 42, is a shoemaker who was recommended to Debi by a close friend, who claimed he was terrific at repairing aerobic shoes. Debi's breath was taken away immediately by the rough way Earl handled her shoes— ripping the laces out, yanking the tongue back and exposing the inner sole. This was a man who knew something about shoes and wasn't ashamed to show it.

When Debi came back a week later to pick them up, Earl noticed her biceps, and asked her out shark fishing. She agreed, and they spent a wonderful after-noon on Earl's trawler. That evening as the sun was setting, they filleted and grilled a hammerhead while polishing off a couple of bottles of Chardonnay.

Debi was infatuated with Earl's knowledge of the deep and his expertise at baiting hooks. She wasn't dis-appointed when he proved equally wonderful in bed.

The following weekend Debi invited Earl over for some low-impact mat work and pasta. Everything was going beautifully—until Earl excused himself to go to the bathroom and returned wearing a taffeta cocktail dress. Debi liked the dress but had mixed feelings about Earl wearing it. Earl was hurt and confused by her response. "Is it the color?" Earl asked quietly. Debi found herself laughing out loud, which incited Earl to angry words about the cost of the dress and Debi's lack of appreciation. He stormed out, forgetting his purse.

In the days that followed, Debi was troubled by the incident. Earl was such an interesting man, she thought, but that dress! She found herself straining her body in workouts, and finally pulled a metatarsal ligament. That's when she came to our office, perplexed and limping.

We told her that Earl could probably be a lot of fun if she could let go of her rigid concepts of the male role in our society. After all, we pointed out, she was a bodybuilder. If she could have massive deltoids, why couldn't Earl wear a dress occasionally? She agreed, her metatarsal improved and she returned Earl's purse. Now, Debi enjoys his company *and* his extensive collection of accessories, finding in Earl a man she can respect and a woman she can confide in.

THE SUGAR DADDY—Great Gifts, Good Meals, Bad Sex • Lauren Z., 25, is a second-generation Armenian, doing graduate work in agriculture for arid climates. She has been commended for her courageous experiments grafting mangos with prickly cactus in hopes of creating a unique dessert food crop.

As with most students, Lauren's finances were limited. Her dedication to work left little time to earn extra money for the "fun" things in life: restaurants, vacations, electrolysis. While on a field trip to Brazil, she met Dolf S., a wealthy pie manufacturer and world traveler.

Their eyes met across a smoky cantina and Dolf sent a wonderful bottle of champagne. They toasted, they talked, they danced beneath a bold Brazilian moon. Dolf picked up the check and Lauren with equal ease.

The limo swept them to his hotel. More champagne, music, and with the lights of Brazil shimmering out the window, Lauren had the most disappointing sexual experience of her life. Dolf was flatulent during sex. He kept apologizing, but the more vigorous their sex, the louder the emissions from his buttocks.

Lauren was relieved when he finally achieved orgasm with one long sustained burst and rolled over in a deep snore. Vulgar noises always seemed to be emanating from this man, Lauren thought to herself. She had no idea he would be so hairy either. That cluster of dark tufts that covered his back disgusted her. She fell asleep dreaming of buffalo.

In the morning, Dolf had awakened before Lauren and served her a lovely breakfast in bed, complete with

flowers and champagne. Dolf seemed to have no memory of last night's rude cacophony. He smiled as he told of the day he had planned: shopping in Rio, lunch on his yacht and an overnight trip to Tierra del Fuego. When Lauren refused, on the basis of her research responsibilities, Dolf was visibly crestfallen. He asked about the following week, but Lauren said she would have to call him.

Lauren never saw Dolf again, and she has yet to enjoy the comforts of a truly wealthy man. The sex may not have been great and Dolf certainly had a notable problem, but how easy it would have been for Lauren to become "a friend," an occasional traveling companion who helped Dolf use his money with imagination. Every picture has its own little moustache, but let's not ignore the face value.

THE EGO MANIAC • Miriam C., 46, is the editor of a successful business magazine written in Japanese. She thought she had seen her share of over-sized egos until she spotted Colin P. at the beach trying to walk on water. When she questioned his efforts, he barked back, "Ocean's polluted. No one could walk on this stuff."

Miriam was amazed by his total confidence, his unflagging belief in his eminent greatness and his uncanny ability to relate the subject of any conversation to *his* achievements—which began with his birth.

They spent hours at Colin's house, a fantastic six-story structure whose indoor swimming pool was shaped

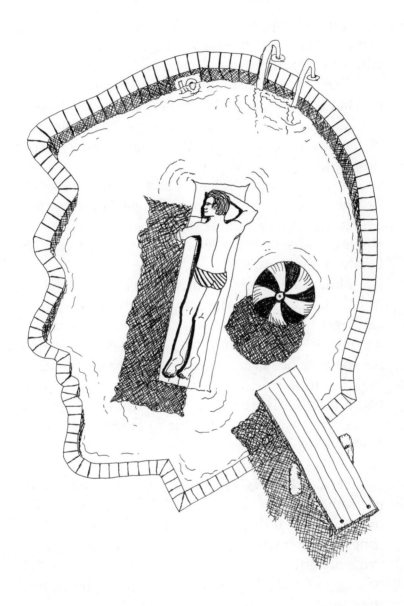

in the form of Colin's profile. Strolling down the wind-
ing driveway, whose twists and turns formed his name

in script, Colin would often point to the oversized vanity plates on his DeLorean saying, "If someone doesn't know who you are, tell them . . . again and again!"

Cited by an officer for going the wrong way on a one-way street, Colin refused to pay the ticket and fought city hall until they acquiesced and changed the direction of the street. Not to be outdone, he promptly began driving the opposite way.

After awhile, Miriam found Colin's obsessive behavior interfered with her breathing, and thought it best to quit seeing him. A month later he noticed her absence and sent her a letter saying he was glad she finally saw it his way.

Miriam admitted to us that it was nice never having to hold up her end of the conversation, and she could easily get her work done while Colin rattled on about his dreams, his plans, himself. Also, he never criticized her, because he never focused on her for longer than it took her to nod her head in agreement with what he had just said. "There was a certain freedom in it," she sighed, "but when he asked me to crown him king of Norway—well, that was the last straw."

THE PERFECTIONIST • "It's never right unless he does it," said Anna K., 34, as we worked to restore feeling in her wrists and hands. She had been hanging by her wrists for several hours a day hoping to make her arms longer and thinner—more perfect. "He belongs in France, where disdain is a national pastime," she continued.

Anna, a top furrier in Manhattan's garment district, was referring to Charles D., a 44-year-old official in the Dept. of Weights and Measurements. They had been dating for several months after meeting in line at the drug store where Charles was buying a quantity of sterile gauze to line his kitchen drawers.

Anna liked him immediately. He was neat, sensitive and spoke English. She invited Charles over for dinner. He arrived bearing a bouquet of orchids and a box of truffles. Anna was delighted when he offered to help with dinner. At first, he was just making the salad, but then he insisted the veal needed a little tenderizing, next it was an exquisite little sauce that he threw together from scratch—in short, Charles made dinner while Anna fetched utensils, ran to the store for capers and checked his answering service.

After dinner, Charles rearranged her spices—by geographical origin—moving down the globe from north to south. After dusting the stereo, they went to bed together, but lovemaking was interrupted by Charles' sudden concern for the fiber count in Anna's sheet.

"I find it difficult to be aroused on a blend," Charles said flatly.

He spent the rest of the evening rearranging her books by color and size, and then moved on to her drawers as Anna fell into a troubled sleep.

She awoke the next morning to the sound of Charles directing the installation of a new dishwasher.

"That old one leaves unsanitary spots that could be the disaster of any dinner party," he intoned. "The refrigerator will be here at nine, but I've got my weekly appointment to have my ears cleaned." He pecked her on the cheek and left the number of a personal fitness instructor taped to her bathroom mirror.

"I kept thinking he was special—unlike other men," Anna told us. "It was just so nice to be with a man who

put the seat down that I guess I didn't mind so much when he suggested cosmetic surgery."

Charles encouraged Anna to have her nose made smaller, her breasts enlarged, her thighs reduced and her ear lobes bobbed. "When he said my arms were too short I started to feel that I might never look right for him. While I was hanging from the chin up bar he put up in my doorway, he began scrutinizing my feet. When he hinted at binding them I was infuriated and told him that his teeth were irregularly spaced and his nose hair was offensive. He left saying he could never be with someone who used that tone of voice."

That was the last time Anna saw Charles. She should have known that Charles's quest for perfection was endless and could never be fulfilled, no matter what she did. If she had taken into account that most of the changes she felt he imposed on her were things she really wanted to change about herself she would have been less exasperated with Charles and simply said no—that she was happy with her big feet.

The important thing, once again, is to know you're already perfect and it's just a matter of how *you* want to improve on it.

THE CLAM—He'll never open up ● Rachel O., 35, executive operator for a long distance telephone company, began seeing Lester F., 51, the security guard in the lobby of her office building. Lester informed us that Rachel had been attracted to his quiet demeanor and the way he used to touch her hand when she took the pencil to sign out.

Apparently, after long hours eavesdropping on other people's phone conversations, Rachel was happy to have a lover of her own—even if Lester didn't talk much and rarely moved.

At first, quiet evenings in front of the TV were enough. Lester was warm and his regular breathing soothed Rachel. But when Rachel insisted they get out one night and go to the mall, Lester wouldn't budge. Rachel began questioning him, "Don't you ever want to talk about things?"

"What things?" Lester would ask.

"Like how was your day?" Rachel coaxed.

"Fine," Lester answered.

"What about my day?" Rachel hinted.

"I don't know," he answered.

"Do you think we get along?" Rachel finally demanded. "Do you think we share anything?"

"I don't know. What do you think?" Lester said as he continued to stare at the TV.

Rachel huffed off to the mall by herself. But as she browsed through the knee-high hosiery section she sensed she wasn't having fun. She ended up buying four pairs of hose in colors she would never wear. She felt angry, alone and overcharged.

Unable to control herself, Rachel drove to Lester's and pounded on his front door until he opened it. "I was molested by a roving gang of Irish youths!" Rachel gasped and fell into his arms. "Well, they tend to get rambunctious this close to St. Paddy's day," Lester said, easing her to the floor. "There's a good Bonanza rerun on," he continued. Rachel could contain herself no longer. "What's the matter with you!" she screamed.

"I don't know, what do you think?" he answered, turning up the volume on the opening of "Bonanza."

Rachel hurled her shopping bag filled with hose at him and left.

The next day, Rachel saw Lester as she was signing out from work. He didn't say anything about the night before. As a matter of fact, he didn't say anything at all. Instead of signing her name, Rachel wrote "Good-bye." When Lester reminded her to put the time down, Rachel jammed the pencil through Lester's hand.

The relationship was pretty much over. Rachel went through a lot of guilt about her actions. Lester still has difficulty grasping things. That's when we met him. Once again, it seems that Rachel was the one who had expectations that simply did not match reality.

Lester's lack of conversation or enthusiasm for most human activities should have made Rachel feel free to do whatever she wanted. Lester could have been a sort of prop she could place in any room. She could have thought of Lester as a large cat that was potty trained. We all know how pets improve one's health and life expectancy. Lester may not have been the perfect mate, but he could have been a more than adequate doorstop.

THE MAN WHO HATES WOMEN •
Margaret, a wan, attractive 43-year-old optometrist, was immediately attracted to Dean, 38, a pro at an all-male tennis club. She was excited by his aloof gaze, his slightly cocky body language, his self-satisfied grin. So, when Dean asked her out for a night at the roller-derby, Margaret was thrilled.

He had scarcely picked her up for their date when the trouble began. First, he caught Margaret's thumb in the car door as he closed it for her. Then he nearly strangled her as he helped her on with the shoulder harness. At the restaurant, Dean pulled Margaret's chair out too far and chuckled under his breath as she toppled to the floor (causing a pelvic trauma that needed treatment later). When he "accidentally" bumped her into the path of an oncoming pack at the roller rink, Margaret became suspicious.

As Dean helped her apply ice to her swollen ankle, neck and hand, Margaret asked, "I don't mean to pry, but . . . are you angry with me?" Dean's eyes filled with rage as he threw the compress across the room.

"Since you asked, Margaret," he sneered, "yes, I *am* angry. I hate your soft skin, your curvaceous body, your manicured nails, you high-heeled shoes. Most of all, I hate your intelligence. In short, Margaret—I hate you because you are . . . a . . . woman."

Margaret, a woman in love (if a little short-sighted), was determined to turn Dean around. She began to speak in a low voice, started smoking cigars, and bought a selection of summer and winter trousers. When we met her, her body was totally askew, and she walked like John Wayne in a tube skirt.

We helped her regain her natural gait without resorting to gender confusion and set about repairing her relationship with Dean. We pointed out that, because Dean hated ALL women, there was little chance of him cheating on her. Also, his outwardly hostile and psychopathic behavior kept Margaret's shrewish mother at a distance, allowing Margaret a freedom she had wished for all her life.

By working together, Dean and Margaret have reached a separate peace. She sports a boyish new haircut and several layers of protective clothing, while he

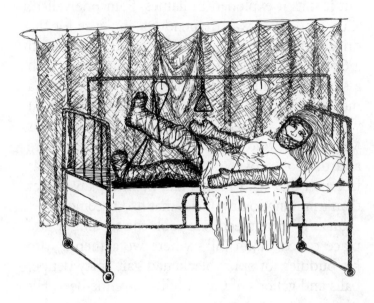

has grown as a person, no longer hating only women, but beagles and Methodists as well.

THE MAN'S MAN • Robin C., 30, winced through our office doors with a dislocated shoulder from the recoil of a twelve gauge shotgun.

"Skeet shooting—ouch!" she explained as we popped the ball back into the socket. She went into more detail as we applied Absorbine Jr. to the sore shoulder.

"I work in an antique store. On my way home I noticed a camera crew was set up on the street. Suddenly, a car came squealing around the corner at high speed and flipped over several times. Amazingly, it landed on its wheels and the driver leaped out just as it exploded in flames. Someone yelled, 'Cut!' and there was tremendous applause for the driver of the car as he dusted himself off and chugged a Coke. He was handsome, in a rugged way, with a smudge on his cheek, a gleam in his eye and a metal plate in his head. I couldn't help myself—I walked over and shook his hand. His name was Mac, and he told me he had to set himself on fire and dive off a twelve-story building, but if I was free after that . . . ? I said I had no firm plans, other than trimming some cuticles that had become rather coarse. It was agreed. He took me to dinner at a place called Cajun Bill's where we gathered with his buddies for spicy blackened gar, spicy pepper balls and gallons of Cajun Bill's Cayenne Beer. His friends were boisterous, loquacious and sloppy, but it was all a refreshing change from the antique business. Normally, at that hour I would be sipping sherry and discussing a new purchase of Wedge-wood. This was new and exciting—men drinking, belching, pummeling each other with beer mugs.

Cajun Bill's spicy food had me perspiring pro-fusely, but perspiration never stopped a man like Mac. He drove his Bronco up onto the front steps of my co-op. Before I could say a word, he had me out of the truck and over his shoulder as he climbed the trellis. He opened the second floor window and tossed me on the bed. Unfortunately, it was not my bedroom, but my upstairs neighbor's and they were in it at the time. But I appreciated the drama of the whole thing, and later found myself laughing about it in my kitchen with Mac and a few of his buddies who had dropped by after leaving Cajun Bill's. I fell asleep as Mac and his buddies played poker and emptied my refrigerator.

The next morning I awoke to the smell of bacon, coffee and gunpowder. Downstairs I found Mac and his buddies making breakfast and handloaded shotgun shells in preparation for a little skeet shooting. I was flattered when Mac invited me to come along—even though I was a little disappointed when the guys all piled in the front and I was forced to ride in the back of the pick-up. Mac said it was safer back there. As we drove along I could hear the guys laughing and talking, occasionally firing their shotguns out the window of the truck. I began to wonder if Mac and I would ever spend any time alone.

When we arrived at SKEET 'N STUFF, Mac seemed to know everybody and they were all guys. I realized if I was ever going to hold Mac's attention I'd have to prove myself to be as good as his buddies, or at least wear lots of plaid. I made a bold gesture and grabbed one of the numerous shotguns littering the hood of the truck. I fired at random, hitting a tree, the ground and the snack bar before realizing the recoil from the shotgun had dislocated my shoulder. I decided then and there to see a good chiropractor and to stop seeing Mac."

Robin's situation is not uncommon. Many women find themselves with men who prefer the company of men. Though this can be an obstacle to fulfilling certain needs, we shouldn't let it get in the way of a possible "user friendly relationship." Mac and his buddies could be handy when it comes to moving furniture or tarring the roof. Think not in terms of attention, but in terms of "manpower"—some real can-do muscle to get those dirty jobs done. Also, Robin would have been wise to begin her shooting with a smaller gauge, or perhaps even a BB gun, and gradually work her way up to the twelve gauge. Shooting can be fun if you have the proper instruction . . . and a good lawyer.

Chapter Four

COMPLEXES—
They're Really Not

"Complex" is a term grossly over-used in the realm of psychotherapy. The Electra Complex, the Inferiority Complex, the Guilt Complex, the Oedipal Complex—what's so complex about sleeping with your mother? That's just plain sick. We in the chiropractic profession prefer thinking of complexes as "reflexes." We're not talking about psychological problems, we're talking *physical* ones. You see, reflexes are simply the reactions our bodies have to the stupid people around us. Our insights into the following complexes can save you thousands of dollars in needless therapy and prescription drugs, as you realize how wonderfully simple life with the emotionally and mentally crippled can be.

THE CARTOON COMPLEX—
When Animated Characters Take
Over Your Life

The Peter Pan Syndrome, The Wendy Dilemma, The Cinderella Complex, The Snow White Syndrome, each of these books is evidence of a raging national hallucination we've named The Cartoon Complex.

The Cartoon Complex occurs as people become confused in an increasingly complicated world, and reach out for the simplicity of a cartoon kingdom where mice are monogamous and a bunch of dwarves living with a teenage runaway epitomize the nuclear family.

Seduced by best-selling books into the strange reality of Wendy and Peter Pan, we begin to see cartoon characters all around us—the subtle shadings of personality disappear as men become one-dimensional parodies from bad fairy tales. Husbands, bosses, teachers,

Complexes—They're Really Not   **47**

bus drivers, leering at us in twisted technicolor terror. Scary? You bet, but didn't we all have fun seeing "Fantasia" as a child, even though the part with the big devil-looking guy and all the ghosts scared us? Of course we did—and that's precisely why these relationships should be enjoyed for the movies they are, rather than the real-life nightmares the books tell you they are.

Take a look at these favorites from the wonderful world of The Cartoon Complex and see if they sound familiar to you.

TINKERBELL • He's that flashy, gorgeous, gay guy you love and hope to change. He fills your life with frivolous fun: parties, paté and people. You stay up for hours talking about your shared favorite subject—men. One night you find yourself hoping that he'll look in your eyes and kiss you, instead, he asks you where you got your eyeshadow. Careful, they say, Tinkerbell will break your heart. But look on the bright side—look *beyond* the Cartoon Complex. Your plants never looked better! You've learned to pronounce Martinique, and shopping for bargains has become a respected science. So what if there's pixie dust everywhere?

PRINCE CHARMING • The perpetual nice guy, this lover's attentiveness is as suffocating as a wet down comforter. He sends you flowers and a get-well card when all you've done is had your teeth cleaned. He can't stop asking you if everything's all right: "Would you like some more, is it too loud, too cold, too hot, too hard, too soft, too . . . anything?" After awhile, though, the tights in the shower get to be too much. But wait!

Your mom thinks he is a king and, admit it, after a tough day at the office, it's nice to have someone cut up your meat.

PINOCCHIO • A cute bod, Italian looks and a flair for hats hides a chronic liar with a balsa-wood heart. After a couple of months with this guy, you're ready to trim off his rough edges with a chainsaw. But don't be hasty—he's wonderful at lying to people you don't want to talk to on the phone, and in a pinch, he makes great firewood.

SNEEZY • A coke fiend who tells you his sniffles are from allergies. The only thing this drip is allergic to is marriage. However, having this high-energy live-in around can be a great way to save money on large-scale home repairs; a few good snorts and your floors have been sanded, stained and lacquered. With a little encouragement, and a minor investment on your part, skylights pop into the roof, bathroom tile is re-grouted, and your furniture never stops moving until it finds the perfect resting place.

CAPTAIN HOOK • Leather hip boots, long hair and "dirty" nautical talk used to be a turn-on, but now things seem to be getting out of hand. He left you tied to the mast in his living room for over an hour while he went out for fish and chips. His fake tatoos have a tendency to fade and run on your clothes, and you're getting seasick from his waterbed. Hang in there, matey! His ruffled blouses look great with your evening pants and his drop earrings are *fabulous*. The guy's worth an occasional rope burn for his wardrobe alone.

BAMBI • He tells you about all the pain he's been through, beginning with that flimsy story about how his mother was shot when he was a baby (where's the police report?), then the forest fire—a world-class victim. Sensitivity is one thing, but you may think that whimpering when a cab doesn't stop for you is taking it a little too far. On the positive side, he's great on a nature hike, knows all the best watering holes and, weak as he may seem, he is capable of standing on his own four feet. But perhaps best of all, he looks so festive hitched to that sleigh on your roof at Christmas.

THE CHAMELEON COMPLEX— Accepting Yourself For Who He'd Like You To Be, or It's OK To Say Yes!

The Chameleon Complex refers to a pattern of behavior in which the man requests the woman to change according to his moods, whims and social status. When the woman resists, quarrels, bitterness, and, in some cases, dismemberment result. Therapists describe this as a sign of an unhealthy relationship. But we feel chameleons can teach us a lot: versatility, imagination and the ability to wear any color well. Our motto is "Be happy, be a phony!" Here are some "shades" men commonly look for in their women. Go ahead, humor him! The world is a stage and don't forget, you're the leading lady.

THE MYSTERY WOMAN • The film noir effect can be achieved by speaking with a husky voice, speaking in monosyllables only and using words from foreign languages like, "sí," "ciao" and "croissant." Don't shave your legs or under your arms, smoke lots of cigarettes and look bored. It will drive him wild *and* you get to change your name from "Ruth" to "CoCo."

THE HOOKER • Get sleazy. Buy some used fishnets, nine-inch mules and the push-up bra of death.

Walk up and down the sidewalk in front of your house, and when he pulls into the driveway say, "Hey, baby, want some company?" Charge him a lot—by the end of the year, you should have enough to open your own theme park.

THE BODY BUILDER • It can be long, hard work to develop the perfect physique for your man, so it is best to rely on props. Fashion speaks especially loudly, so have your personal shopper settle in at Jane Fonda's to purchase some mix and match lycra day-to-evening wear. This stuff should be *tight*—you'll want as much help as you can get holding those body parts in. Keep that pulsing, work-out beat blasting from your boom box with a collection of tapes by Black family groups. Always have a spray bottle of water handy for instant "sweat." Dab a little Ben Gay at pulse points. Limp occasionally.

THE WOMAN'S WOMAN • Don't worry, it's easy to fool the man who's turned on by watching women *inamorata*. If the idea completely repulses you, you can always get a man you're attracted to to help you out—have him dress in drag for your on-stage bedroom performance—and you'll have some fun too. Or, mirror your bedroom from top to bottom and try to get by with kissing your reflection a lot. Remember that accouterments are important in creating that special lesbian atmosphere, as is personal appearance. Keep framed photos of Gertrude Stein placed strategically around the house, and get a really, *really* bad short haircut. Also, gain weight, lose your sense of humor and stop wearing make-up. That ought to do it!

THE WAIF • There's something appealing (albeit annoying) about a frail, helpless young thing. Mia Farrow, Jean Seberg, Laraine Newman—all these women have capitalized on their own special brand of anemia appeal, and you can too! Simply buy one over-sized sweater and dress it up with a few moth holes and a long, gauzy skirt. Next, hitchhike in the rain with a puppy (no collar) in your arms. Leave poetry books in the bathroom. Put daisies in the tailpipe of his car.

THE RICH BITCH • Overdress. Wear big hair and big jewelry and big teeth and complain about the food at Betty Ford's.

THE PRETTY YOUNG THING • Ask him for help with your homework. Use "really" twice in every sentence. Pretend you don't know who the Beatles are. Pout.

THE OLDER WOMAN • Drink bourbon— straight. Wear hats. Stop moisturizing.

THE BLONDE • Peroxide is too permanent—tomorrow he may want a redhead. Keep a wig handy or, in a pinch, tape a photo of Rutger Hauer to your head.

THE MOTHER • Marry his father.

THE APARTMENT COMPLEX

This is a relative newcomer on the complex scene. It occurs when a growing number of singles seek the perfect dwelling before they allow themselves to find the perfect relationship. For example, Carla M., now 47, had her first apartment at the age of 22. She felt her modest but tidy studio wasn't appropriate for entertaining and decided to hold off serious dating until she could afford a leather, four-piece sectional with matching ottoman.

Unfortunately, by the time she had that accomplished, she soon began seeing a wealthy vegetarian who refused to sit on anything that once had a face. And so it went, Carla acquiring apartment after apartment, each one more fabulous than the last, each one an attempt to cater to the needs of the current object of her affection. In every case, by the time the apartment was decorated to the man's tastes, the man had moved on.

Now Carla is living in an opulent, twenty-two-room mansion, each room decorated in a different theme, from colonial ranch, to nouveau bedouin, to Navajo chic. But alas, her current beau prefers the great outdoors and extended trips in his Winnebago.

Carla could have avoided this expensive cycle and escaped this complex simply by going to the man's apartment. Remember, there's no place like home—*his*.

Chapter Five

THE MOTHER LODE

What Mom Told You to Do

Take a dime –

Buy a nice dress –

Sex? Don't do it –

Get married –

Marry a rich man –

Never call a man –

Meet a nice college boy –

Mind your Ps and Qs –

Be a good hostess –

Never tell your real age –

Always wear clean underwear –

Never overstay your welcome –

Stand up straight –

Keep your legs crossed –

Who's going to buy the cow
if he can get the milk for free –

What You Do

Take your own car –

Buy nice lingerie –

Ask to see test results –

Go into business –

Marry a man who has a job –

Never call a married man at home –

Tutor college boys –

Learn contract law –

Know the good restaurants –

Take aerobics –

Keep a spare in your purse –

Leave before the wife gets home –

Wear a push-up bra –

Keep your fingers crossed –

Why brand one bull when
you can have the whole herd –

Chapter Six

ATTACK OF THE VICIOUS CIRCLE— The Work Addiction

Picture a successful, self-assured woman sporting a stylish maillot and a perfect tan as she swims her way across a blue lagoon—suddenly, without warning, a fin appears behind her. She doesn't see it. The fin glides closer. She senses something and turns her head, but it's too late—she is viciously attacked! Not by a shark, but by her own insatiable lust for perfection. That's right, perfection can be a vicious circle that attacks without warning.

Not a pretty sight, but one we have seen again and again, like eerie metaphysical sequels to "Jaws" or "Friday The 13th." Over-achieving women must beware of this unrestrained passion to constantly perfect *everything* they touch.

Regina D., 28, arrived at our office with the unmistakable signs of a vicious circle attack: enlarged ears from extended telephone calls, swollen fingertips on the right hand from constant calculator activity, elongated left arm from lugging a stuffed briefcase, and a lacerating vocal tone from skewering subordinates. There was also a raw animal fear in her eyes (or maybe her eyeshadow just clashed with her hair) either way, the situation was critical.

After taking her blood pressure, we packed her in ice and she began her story.

"I was managing the trading department at a well-known stock brokerage firm. We had already lost a couple of our top guys to the SEC for exchanging information for cheap lunches. So there was plenty of work to go around. As a matter of fact, I barely found the time to effectively chew my morning croissant, let alone date. My work began to take over my life completely, and when I say completely I mean I had a ticker tape in my shower."

"Who installed it?" We asked, since both of us play the market heavily.

"The company!" she lashed out. We added more ice. "Anyway," she continued, "the pressure was relentless. I needed to find a release before I lost my mind. I told the other women in the office how I felt. They jokingly suggested I try phone sex. You know those numbers you call and a guy answers and you have an erotic conversation?" We both nodded our heads.

"Well, I thought, what the heck, I'll give it a shot—it was only two bucks and I could write it off as a business related expense. So I called—it was 976 something, I forget. Anyway, the phone

rang and rang until finally some guy named Dick answered gruffly and then proceeded to put me on hold for forty-five minutes—I couldn't believe it!

I would have hung up, but the longer I stayed on the more outraged I became. After ten minutes there was no way I was going to hang up without giving the manager of the company a piece of my mind. When Dick picked up again, I demanded to speak with the manager. When he got on the line I told him how long I had been kept waiting, and how it would certainly damage any customer's satisfaction, especially the busy working woman with only a few precious minutes to spare for a little hot talk. He agreed, apologized and belched. He apologized again and encouraged my input.

I suggested he upgrade the operation—hire a polite, well-spoken staff that offered a menu of sexual fantasies to choose from—maybe a daily 'special' as well as a 'package discount' that would make bulk buying attractive and a good gift idea. I told him he was limiting his market by catering only to the English speaking population—why not Spanish, Japanese, Persian? They have needs too.

He loved the idea and offered me an immediate salary to implement my ideas. I couldn't help myself and took it. My work load doubled, then tripled. I stopped sleeping and just fainted occasionally instead.

In just a few months I created an international phone-sex network for men and women that offered travel packages, anonymous singles weekends, and kinky-request-of-the-month awards. Sure it was fun for those who had the time to enjoy it, but I was

too busy *perfecting* it to take any pleasure in it—
the story of my life."

We advised Regina that whenever she felt the urge
to begin perfecting someone or something she should
take a little nap instead—a ten or twenty minute snooze
can quiet the nerves and take the edge off that inner
pressure to perfect. In some extreme cases we've found
that wiring the jaws together may be necessary for the
first months but after that the "naps" should suffice.
One warning. Nancee C., a 37-year-old lighting tech-
nician for "The Love Boat," allowed herself to begin
"power napping"—that is, taking naps at the homes of
powerful and influential people—using it to gain famil-
iarity, sympathy and blankets, but she regularly woke
up to find herself more tired than when she went to
sleep. It was just another "attack of the vicious circle."

Chapter Seven

OUR BODIES OUR CELLS— Finding the Snooze Alarm on Your Biological Clock

As busy Ows go about their busy lives, it is not uncommon for them simply to forget to have children. One day they wake up with hot flashes and a tasteful wardrobe, realizing the only pitter patter they'll ever hear will be the squirrels eating out of the rain gutters of their renovated townhouses. Then, the panic sets in and every available man becomes little more than a walking sperm bank to these reproductively desperate women.

Why let your biological clock push you into a bad relationship? Why take nine months out of your over-crowded schedule when you can experience the joy of motherhood without the hassle? Remember, keeping your options open and getting the fun out of life is what this book is all about. Let's explore some of your options to childbirth, okay? Great!

DATING THE INFANT MAN

This alternative often proves to be the most convenient, as you will find many of the men you date will
display infantile behavior. The "Infant Man" is an emotional baby—needy, whiny and unable to complete many
simple tasks for himself. In this respect he's not unlike
a newborn; however, he is far easier to care for than his
younger counterpart. Grown men can stay at home by
themselves—and if they work "freelance" at anything,
they very often do. Also, they generally don't need braces.
Grown men don't require toilet training, except you do

have to remind them to watch their aim and put the seat down. They can lend you money and cigarettes. And, most helpful during those hectic mornings, they can dress themselves ... well, for the most part. Yet, grown men retain many endearing childlike qualities. So, instead of a baby, opt for that bigger bundle of joy. And, if you don't like him you can always leave him on his own doorstep.

SURROGATE FATHERS—THE NEW DADAISM

There has been a lot in the news lately about surrogate mothers, and it set us to thinking, "Why not surrogate fathers, as well?" At first, it didn't make any sense, but we didn't let that stop us. We began to do some research, which was very difficult since we didn't know where to look, or even what we were looking for. Nevertheless, we went to the library every day and argued with each other about the surrogate father concept. It was during one of these heated arguments that a portly woman named Margo approached us. "Surrogate fatherhood does exist and I am the proof," she whispered. "Also, you are being too loud." Her story was so fascinating that we didn't mind when the librarian told us to leave. Later, at a Bagel Nosh, Margo finished her tale.

"There I was on the brink of facing a childless future—my job at the White House didn't even allow me the time to have sex, let alone raise a family. Then I heard about Dadaism from an old

French maid who was in charge of the presidential tureens.

I took a week off, was artificially inseminated, and began interviewing for a surrogate father. I found Larry, a gardener I had carefully screened for emotional stability and a strong sense of family. When an anonymous letter informed me that Larry had stabbed his sister and grandfather with a rake, I didn't worry—a momentary loss of emotional control was part of being close to the earth—close to nature. I knew Larry was a good man who never had dirt under his nails when he wasn't working, and that he had a certain basic intelligence—I mean he didn't have to think twice when I quizzed him on the difference between annuals and perennials.

The day Timmy, my son, was born I handed him over to Larry to raise until his eighteenth birthday, when he would be returned to me. At that time, I would begin to enjoy the pleasures of a young adult son who could start to look after his mother without making me suffer through the excessive time and energy required during his "difficult years."

Anyway, over the years I was promoted to the upper echelons of government, knowing that Timmy was sharing a rich childhood with his surrogate father—baseball games, pruning shrubs, turning sod—the special times I could never give Timmy. I had to stifle the urge to call, fearing that I might become attached and want to reclaim my son prematurely. But before I knew it, years had passed, and Timmy arrived on my doorstep, a six-foot-tall young man with grass stains on his knees and his

hair trimmed in the shape of a spruce tree. Now,
almost two years later, my yard has never looked
so beautiful, and my life has never been so full."

Margo's is a success story, but the Dada approach can have one prohibitive drawback—surrogate fathers often become attached to the child and have to be assassinated. This can be costly and can have adverse effects on the child. That is why when it comes to Dadaism our motto is "Remember their roots, or we'll shoot!"

Chapter Eight

SEEKING PROFESSIONAL HELP— A Fallacy

Many women find themselves in such a miserable state that even chiropractic doesn't seem enough. They go, sometimes alone, sometimes with their damaged loved ones, to therapists, counselors, psychiatrists, psychologists, social workers and the like, hoping for some instant mental health.

Transsexual Therapists

Beware, therapy has its pitfalls—one of them often being the therapist. Here is the story of Bob and Meredith, who found this out the hard way.

"Bob and I had bought every relationship book there was and we were still right where we started, except that we went into debt adding a library onto the house. Our main problem, though, was that Bob didn't want to be married to me. He wanted my twin brother, Josie, a female impersonator who frequently performed at Bob's Knights of Columbus banquets. The thing was, I didn't want to be married to Bob, either. For years, I had been left to do all the housework and had no time to pursue my own interests. I was tired of it. I know it sounds crazy, but I decided jail was the only answer—I knew in my heart that being a 'lifer' was the only way I would ever get the solitude I needed to read, paint, write and complete my master's degree in sociology. Things reached a breaking point when Bob began introducing Josie as his wife, and I was arrested robbing a 7-11 in my son's Halloween costume.

We went to see Harriet, formerly Hal, a transsexual marriage counselor known for her empathy with both male and female points of view. She put Bob, Josie and me on hormone therapy, and let me tell you, it's been a nightmare. Sure, Bob has become much more "feminine" in his behavior and has begun helping with the household chores, but Josie is no longer impersonating women, he *is* one. Problem is, I've fallen in love with Josie, which is really weird since now we're identical twins, and Bob's fallen for Harriet. Our lives are a mess. We should have learned to work with things the way they were."

So, if you need help, you might take a leaf out of Bob's and Meredith's book: never seek therapy from anyone who has been more than one gender in his or her lifetime.

THE DR. RUTH SYNDROME

"I just wanted a little advice," said Carlotta S., 38, a taxidermist specializing in water fowl. "I wasn't having much of a sex life when I met Keith." (Keith was a chronic game poacher active throughout the northern United States and Canada.)

"I'll never forget him walking into my studio with a smile on his face and an albatross under his coat. He said he found it near a lake. I believed him and did a beautiful job on it. Keith was very happy when he came to pick up the stuffed alba-tross and he asked me for dinner, but before we had even started driving I found myself in the back of his old panel truck necking in the midst of his traps, pelts and hunting gear. I have to say I have rarely enjoyed myself as much, but it did strike me as a little strange when he just dropped me off at my house and said thanks. When I gave Dr. Ruth a call she said, 'Zee man in queztion eez dizplaying sociopathzic behavior and alzo, I find him a little strange. You would do good to avoid any future contact until he has at least paid for zee stuffing of zee albatross or bought you a comparably priced meal.' I thanked Dr. Ruth and continued to watch her show regularly.

The weeks were going by as usual—fall brought a lot of ducks into the shop—and I was stuffing a mallard, when in walked Keith with a large turkey under his coat. He claimed it was for Macy's and he needed it by Friday. I sharply told him he could forget it until he paid me for the albatross, or at least bought me dinner. He lowered his head and left without saying a word. I called Dr. Ruth to tell her how well I had handled the situation. She was very proud of me and found my case interesting enough to be invited on her show.

It was exciting being on TV and talking about sex in such a frank way with other women while millions of people watched. When I told the doctor how much I enjoyed it she suggested that I might start a sex seminar for rural women in my area. I returned home with enthusiasm and a slight German accent.

In the weeks that followed I called women, scheduled meetings and even started a newsletter, called *The Chatterbox*. I didn't think about having sex anymore because I spent all my time talking about it. The more I talked about it, the less I wanted to do it. It all started to unravel when I had

gotten my own local radio show and one of the callers asked me as an afterthought when the last time I'd had sex was—and I couldn't remember. She asked me how I could call myself an authority on something that I rarely practiced. It seemed as if all the months of sex sublimated into talking whooshed down on me and I couldn't get off the air soon enough. I drove out to the woods and began hollering Keith's name. I didn't find him, but I met a widower who was night fishing for perch."

Carlotta began to enjoy sex again. She is busy with her taxidermy business which now has a thriving mail order division and she has even gone out with Keith occasionally. He now offers her game in exchange for her work. She finds that she hardly ever *talks* about sex and does it a lot more these days.

ALTERNATIVES TO THERAPY

Religious Pilgrimages • This is the ideal way to forget your relationship worries and focus on a more pragmatic approach to life. First of all, they take months, so you'll be too busy to reflect endlessly on how to make yourself, or your love life, more perfect. In fact, you won't be able to reflect on anything, except maybe soaking your feet. You'll meet lots of nice, decent people and you'll get to see the world. Jill L., 28, recently completed a three-year trek from Milwaukee, Wisconsin to Meddebemps, Maine.

"I really felt there was something missing in my life and I didn't want to turn to drugs or needlepoint, so I figured God would be the best way to fill the void. I did some research and found out that He was living in Maine, in the form of a retail jeweler. A bunch of members from my investment club and I decided to make the trip on foot, wearing Dr. Scholl's sandals—that way if the guy turned out to be a phony, we'd at least have toned up our legs. The trip took much longer than we thought— eighteen months—none of us can resist a roadside antique shop. By the time the twelve of us reached Meddebemps, we had collected enough artifacts to open the Plymouth Rock Museum and Theme Park.

It was there that I finally met God, who was really Roger, a cubic zirconium specialist whose cheap TV ads had gained him a popularity that snowballed into a cult following. Roger and I fell in love, and are now auditioning for jobs as the permanent hosts of a syndicated evangelical TV show."

Jill, and thousands like her, seem to be on to something. Granted, the burlap robe and thongs can get uncomfortable after awhile, but aren't those trips to the bookstore, to the shrink, to the—dare we say it?—chiropractor, just as chafing?

TRAFFIC SCHOOL • Another handy diversionary technique, traffic school can provide hours of relief from the ouch of Owing. Julie K., 40, has found these hours of driving instruction invaluable to her mental well-being.

"One day, I simply found myself running in circles. I had more self-help books, cassettes and videos than anyone I knew, and I was still spending $300 a month seeing a therapist. I was on my way to a taping of the "Oprah Winfrey Show"—the theme that day was 'Women Who Bludgeon Their Husbands: Stress or Self-Defense'—when I got a speeding ticket. My driving record was spotless, so I went to traffic school to take care of it. Well, it was one of those comedy traffic schools where the teacher makes it fun for you to do your time. It was the best time I'd had in years, so soon I was parking in loading zones, making illegal U-turns,

speeding in radar traps, honking in hospital zones—
I couldn't stop myself. I wanted to repent for my
violations, I wanted to belong . . . I wanted to laugh.
Things reached a head when I intentionally rammed
a highway patrol car."

Julie came to us with whiplash from that dramatic
crash, and the more she shared with us, the more we
were impressed with her creative solution to the self-
help bind. She is now happily married to traffic-school
mogul Saul "Mr. Crack Up" Grenzbach.

CPR TRAINING • While on the self-
improvement kick, why not take a course that will ben-
efit others as well? If you frequently date older men, a
CPR course can give those relationships more staying
power, and what the heck, you never know who you
might meet. Let's take a look at Bobbi, 31, registered

nurse, weekend championship ice skater and CPR class addict:

"I took the first class just to brush up on my paramedic skills, but before I knew it, I was hooked. After my second divorce, real men had become so threatening to me that Raoul—he's our CPR mannequin—actually became an appealing alternative to the losers I seem to attract like flies. I like Raoul's clean-shaven face, his cool, flawless skin, his serene expression, the way his chest gently rises and falls every time his lips touch mine. It's gotten ridiculous—I'm actually jealous when the other students practice on him; all that heavy breathing sends me

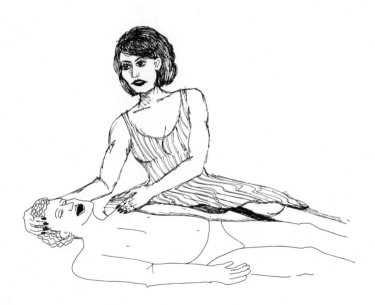

into a frenzy. I know, as I thump and breathe, that Raoul and I can build a life together. Sure, he's just a dummy—but so were my two ex-husbands."

We didn't discourage Bobbi from her infatuation with her laid-back lover, but instead showed her how to prop Raoul up in a chair, thus saving her from the chronic backaches that had been plaguing her since their floor-level courtship began. We hear that things between them are just great, and that their new daughter is a little doll.

Chapter Nine

ANATOMY OF A RELATIONSHIP

Throughout this book we have described the physical symptoms plaguing Ows. We offer you this handy chart to help you pinpoint your own Ow-ness. Remember, these aches and pains can, and should, be used to alert you to the need, not only for chiropractic consultation, but also for reassessing your bleak outlook!

1. Black and blue marks—rolling with the punches

2. Shoulder spasms—reaching too high

3. Pain in the neck—paranoia or oversized pillows

4. Aching cheeks—laughing at too many bad jokes

5. Locked jaw—terminal stress

6. Abdominal cramps—swallowing all that anger

7. Aching knuckles—trying to get a grip

8. Shin splints—running in circles

9. Trick knees—groveling for a raise

10. Pigeon toes—going in two directions at once

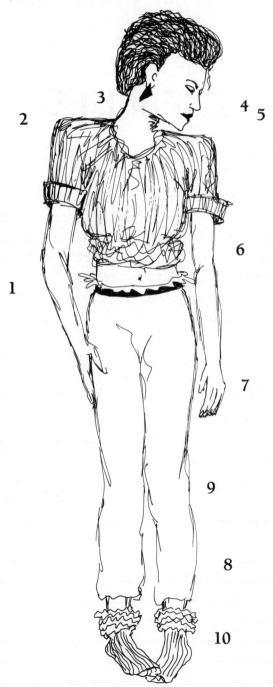

EXERCISES

Now that you've read this book, you've no doubt gained a better insight into yourself, your relationships and the state of male/female interaction in general. These simple exercises are designed to help you assess what you've learned and to put this new knowledge into practice in your life. If you're really bored, re-read your answers when you have finished.

1. Give an accounting of how every moment of your day is spent. (If you have time to make this list you are not an Ow and should disregard everything you have read thus far.)

_____

_____

_____

_____

_____

_____

_____

_____

_____

_____

_____

2. Describe your perfect man. (Hint: This is a trick question.)

_____
_____
_____
_____
_____
_____
_____
_____
_____
_____
_____
_____
_____
_____
_____
_____
_____
_____
_____
_____

3. In Column A, make a list of all the smart women you know. In column B, make a list of all the men you know who are as smart as, or smarter than, the women in column B. (You may not list your father.)

COLUMN A   **COLUMN B**
_____   _____
_____
_____
_____
_____
_____
_____
_____
_____
_____
_____
_____

4. Briefly, describe what women really want from men in these key areas:

romantically:

_____

_____

_____

_____

sexually:

_____

_____

_____

_____

spiritually:

_____

_____

_____

_____

financially:

_____

_____

_____

Now, review your answers and compare them to what women actually get from men. In the space provided below, write an essay on the futility of male/female relationships and how this relates to the high percentage of tranquilizer abuse by today's Over-achieving woman. Try to stay awake until you have completed your answer.

_____

_____

_____

_____

_____

_____

_____

_____

_____

5. What do you see as the role of the chiropractor in caring for the mental and physical well-being of today's women in stress? How much would you be willing to pay for this care? (Please include Group Health Insurance number.)

_____

_____

_____

_____

_____

_____

_____

_____

_____

_____

_____

_____

_____

6. Write your own case history, using the form below. Sell it for big bucks to the author of the next book that claims to help smart women.

Age:
Occupations:
Hobbies:
Children:
Religion:
Married (# of times):
Divorced (# of times):
Loser dates (# to date):
Books purchased (# to date):
Crimes of passion (kind and #):
Muscle spasms (kind and #):